Black's Sketchbooks

London   Adam & Charles Black

PUBLISHED BY
A. & C. BLACK · SOHO SQUARE · LONDON W.

Stratford-on-Avon

A sketch-book

by

Gordon Home

Adam & Charles Black
Soho Square : London

Illustrations

In the High Street.

HOLY TRINITY CHURCH

The Birthplace

The Birthroom
in Shakespeare's Birthplace.

The Guildhall
& Grammar School

Gowper
Howe

The Site of New Place
& the Guild Chapel —

THE NEW PLACE PANELLING
IN THE FALCON HOTEL

GORDON
HOME

A DOORWAY IN SHEEP STREET

THE MEMORIAL THEATRE
FROM THE CHURCHYARD WALL.

GORDON
HOME

THE CLOPTON BRIDGE

THE CORNER OF ELY STREET
HIGH STREET

IN THE HALL OF THE
HARVARD HOUSE

A carved bracket
on the front of
Harvard House

GORDON
HOME

Details of the
front of the
Harvard House

The Approach
to the Church Porch.

In Holy Trinity Church
The Clopton Chapel

Mason's Court
Rother Street.

A Garden View
of the Birthplace.

Seven Gables of
The Dower House

Anne Hathaway's Cottage
at Shottery

The Garden View
of "Anne Hathaway's
Cottage"

"Anne Hathaway's Bed"
— so called · in her cottage
at Shottery.

The home of Mary Arden.
Shakespeare's mother at
Wilmcote

First published in Great Britain in 1913
by A&C Black Publishers
36 Soho Square
London W1D 3QY
www.acblack.com

This edition published 2009

© 1913, 2009 A&C Black

ISBN 978-14081-1122-2

A CIP record of this book is available from the British Library

Printed and bound in China